PASSING THE BUCK

What the Bible Says About Giving

by

DAVID HOCKING

Promise Publishing Co.
Orange, California 92668

Published by Promise Publishing Co.
Orange, California 92668

Cover Design by Mary Chapeau
Photo by Art Zippel
Editor: M.B. Steele

Printed in the United States of America

Scripture quotations, unless otherwise noted, are from the New King James Version, copyright 1979, 1980, 1982 by Thomas Nelson Publishers.

IBSN 0-939497-04-2

Library of Congress, Cataloguing-in Process

PASSING THE BUCK
      Hocking, David

SPECIAL EDITION
FOR
THE BIOLA HOUR

13800 BIOLA AVENUE
LA MIRADA, CALIFORNIA 90639

TABLE OF CONTENTS

chapter one

ARE YOU WILLING TO GIVE?

The Principle of Commitment

Giving to the work of the Lord (or anything else) is not a natural instinct in the human heart. Many good people find they can take part in church, attend meetings, teach Sunday School and bring food for the potluck dinner. But when the offering plate is passed, some people get really up tight. One man declares that every time he has heard me preach at my church, I've preached on giving. I looked back over my notes and realized that he's visited only twice.

It's important to understand "giving" because, in fact, the Bible is not silent on the subject. The very word, "giving", is where we get our English name, Nathan - "Gift of God." The word, Nathan, is used eighteen hundred times in Hebrew. In the New Testament, "didomi" is a common word for "giving." There are other words used, too, but that basic word is used four hundred times.

Over and over again, the Bible associates our money with our commitment and walk with the Lord. Yet in our narcissistic culture, the tendency is to separate our finances from our spiritual lives. We want to tell others how we feel, not what we do. But the Bible says that what you do is a more important barometer of who you are than anything else.

The paper I write on is amoral. The cup we take communion from in church is amoral, also. The hymnbook we sing from is amoral. The microphone I speak into is definitely amoral. But, if I take the microphone and use it to club you, it becomes a moral issue.

Money, too, is amoral. There's no morality connected with it, whatsoever. But, if you let it control you, it becomes a moral issue. You can be totally affected in your Christian life by your money and how you handle it.

You say to me, "In our self-centered culture, I don't want to hear that! I want you to separate for me the stuff of my life from who I am." But the Bible actually will not let us do that. The Bible puts them together. The matter of giving is a most serious Christian issue. Many of us are having problems in our marriages and our families. We are struggling with our individual walk with the Lord over the issue of money and we don't even know that's the problem.

Tithing is not willing giving. There are several words for tithes but tithes are always taxations. Israel was a theocracy and tithing wasn't voluntary. It was required. There are other words for offerings. These can refer to sacrifices or to material possessions that we give. You will also find the words "freewill" or "willing giving" offerings.

Freewill offerings are our subject here. Many good churches are committed to freewill offerings...not taxation...not requirements. They don't even keep records of your giving or names of donors. Some don't even want to know. Supporters give their gifts and responsibile leaders spend it for the work of the Lord. These churches are built on the principle of freewill offerings.

As you know from watching television, listening to the radio or from going to some churches, Christian enterprises are in trouble in the area of giving. What they are teaching about giving is often very wrong and we must say, "Wait a minute! What does the Bible tell us?"

I Chronicles 29 is a great chapter about the building of the temple. But along with the story of the building, there is a challenging picture of commitment and willingness to give that comes through clearly. This well-known chapter tells us the story of a great effort - raising money for the most beautiful structure of the ancient world, the Temple of God. As we read the text, six special attitudes strike us as being characteristic of the people involved in this building project.

AFFECTION

Furthermore King David said to all the congregation: "My son, Solomon, whom alone God has chosen, is young and inexperienced; and the work is great, because the temple is not for man but for the Lord.

"Now for the house of my God I have prepared with all my might: gold for things to be made of gold, silver for things of silver, bronze for things of bronze, iron for things of iron, wood for things of wood, onyx stones, stones to be set, glistening stones of various colors, all kinds of precious stones, and marble slabs in abundance.

"Moreover, because I have set my affection on the house of my God, I have given to the house of my God, over and above all that I have prepared for the holy house, my own special treasure of gold and silver"(vss.1-3).

CONSECRATION

"Who then is willing to consecrate himself this day to the Lord?" Then the leaders of the father's houses, leaders of the tribes of Israel, the captains of thousands and of hundreds, with the officers over the king's work, offered willingly. They gave for the work of the house of God."(vss.5-7).

REJOICING

Then the people rejoiced, for they had offered willingly, because with a loyal heart they had offered willingly to the Lord; and King David also rejoiced greatly. Therefore David blessed the Lord before all the congregation; and David said:

"Blessed are You, Lord God of Israel,
our Father, forever and ever.
Yours, O Lord, is the greatness,
The power and the glory,
The victory and the majesty;
For all that is in heaven
and in earth is Yours;
Yours is the kingdom, O Lord,
And You are exalted as head over all.
Both riches and honor come from You,
And You reign over all.
In Your hand is power and might;
In Your hand it is to make great
And to give strength to all.
Now therefore, our God,
We thank You
And praise Your glorious name"(vss.9-13).

WILLINGNESS

"But who am I, and who are my people,
That we should be able to offer
so willingly as this?
For all things come from You,
And of Your own we have given You.
For we are aliens and pilgrims before You.
As were all of our fathers;
Our days on earth are as a shadow,
And without hope.

"O Lord, our God, all this abundance that we have prepared to build You a house for Your holy name is from Your hand, and is all Your own"(vss.14-16).

UPRIGHTNESS

"I know also, my God, that You test the heart and have pleasure in uprightness. As for me, in the uprightness of my heart I have willingly offered all these things; and now with joy I have seen Your people, who are present here to offer willingly to You. O Lord God of Abraham, Isaac, and Israel, our fathers, keep this forever in the intent of the thoughts of the heart of Your people, and fix their heart toward You...to keep Your commandments and Your testimonies and Your statutes, to do all these things, and to build the temple for which I have made provision"(vss.17-19).

COMMITMENT

Then David said to all the congregation, "Now bless the Lord your God." So all the congregation blessed the Lord

God of their fathers, and bowed their heads and prostrated themselves before the Lord and the king. So they ate and drank before the Lord with great gladness on that day(vss.20,22).

A PRAYER FOR WILLINGNESS IN GIVING

Father, help us to focus on what it is to give willingly to You that we might honor You in our lives. I pray for those who have never begun to give anything to You. Perhaps they have never received the free gift of Your salvation and eternal life nor come to believe that Jesus died on the cross for their sin, and rose again from the dead. God, help them to know that He gave His life for us. Then we ask You to show us how that affects our giving to You.

In Jesus' name we pray. Amen.

introduction

There are seven basic facts which a person who knows how to give willingly to God understands. This produces in that person the attitudes we have just read about in David's day. It is not by chance that one believer knows how to give to God and another does not. There is an understanding in the heart of one that is lacking in the other. Let's see if we can identify what those seven mighty truths are.

* * * * * * * * * * * * * *

UNDERSTAND THAT THE WORK IS FOR GOD NOT FOR MAN

If you can give willingly to God, there are seven things that are true of you. First of all and above all, you realize that the work is done for God and not for man. Everyone who gives willingly understands that. When you feel that you are required to give, your heart is not in it. You have no desire to give. But when you give willingly, it's because you are giving to the Lord, not to man. You realize that the work your gifts support is for the Lord, not for man.

Look again at I Chronicles 29:1. The last phrase says,

"...because the temple is not for man, but for the Lord God."

If you give willingly, the very first thing that is true of you is that you know the work is for the Lord, it is not for man. That motivates you to give.

Haggai 1:2-7 says,

"Thus speaks the Lord of hosts, saying: 'This people says, "The time has not come, the time that the Lord's house should be built."'" Then the word of the Lord came by Haggai the prophet, saying, "Is it time for you yourselves to dwell in your paneled houses, and this temple to lie in ruins?" Now therefore, thus says the Lord of hosts: "Consider your ways!

> *"You have sown much, and bring in little;*
> *You eat, but do not have enough;*
> *You drink, but you are not filled with drink;*
> *You clothe yourselves, but no one is warm;*
> *And he who earns wages,*
> *Earns wages to put into a bag with holes."*

" Thus says the Lord of hosts:

CONSIDER YOUR WAYS!"

There are a lot of us having problems financially because the bag we're putting our money in, has a hole in it and it's getting bigger. What we earn is falling through and our paycheck is spent before we get it. Why? Because the work of the Lord is not number one to us.

It doesn't matter how much money you make, you can get into trouble. The higher the salaries go, the worse the problems are. More money doesn't bring happiness. We already know that. It's a "bag with holes," God said. Money is slipping through your fingers and you don't even realize it because you're concentrating on what YOU are doing rather than focusing on the work of the Lord.

Does the work of the Lord come first? "Oh, yes!" you say. Perhaps you don't realize what is really involved and what

that means. Only when you believe that the work is actually
for the Lord and not for man are you motivated to give. You
have to keep checking to be sure the work of the Lord is
prominent in your life.

Haggai is saying, "The temple of God is lying in waste and
you're concentrating on your own beautiful homes! Something is wrong." It's very difficult to give as God wants us to
- with a willing heart - when the work of the Lord is not important to us. We start the new habit of giving willingly by
realizing that...

THE WORK IS FOR THE LORD, NOT FOR MAN

* * * * * * * * * * * * *

DECIDE TO LOVE THE WORK OF THE LORD

In verse three of I Chronicles 29, David says,

*"Moreover, because I have set my affection on the house
of God, I have given to the house of my God over and above
all I prepared."*

The principle here is very simple. Willing giving comes
from a heart that loves the work of the Lord. Let me ask you
a question, "Do YOU love the work of the Lord? When a
missionary writes and tells you about a need, do you love
God's work so much you just can't wait to find the money
somewhere and send it to them?"

David said he's done this "...because I have set my affection on the house of my God, I have given to the house of my
God, over and above all that I have prepared." If you give
willing offerings, it's because you love the work of the Lord.

The Psalmist repeats his love for the house of the Lord
many times. "I love the house of the Lord." "I was glad when

they said unto me, 'Let us to into the house of the Lord.'" "I love God's temple so much that I want to bring my offerings to Him and bless Him and exalt His name." Throughout the Psalms, we find that sentiment expressed consistently over and over again.

Do YOU love the work of God? Do you really? I believe that is important when you give to God. There is great joy in giving to the Lord when you love God's work. Is it really important to you that Jesus said that we are to make disciples of all nations? Have you decided to commit your time, energy, life and family to achieve that objective or do you dole out to God only what you think is necessary?

In Christian teaching today, we are told over and over again, "If you give this, you will get that." We're being told that financial prosperity is important. However, earthly treasures are nothing compared to what heaven is going to contain. The Bible says, "Lay not up for yourselves treasures on earth where moth and rust doth corrupt and thieves break through and steal. But lay up treasures in heaven." Yet, Christian ministries today are telling us that if we give to them, somehow we will prosper materially and be blessed. If we do enjoy prosperity, it adds nothing to our faith. Be very careful about what people are saying today. It's unimportant whether God blesses me financially or not. I want to say, "Thank you" to Him and to honor Him. I love the work of God and I want to see it prosper around the world.

There is wonderful satisfaction for me in doing my job. I really enjoy what I do. And I believe it is important that I do my work as well as I know how. The need to carry out my responsibilities is something I take very seriously. But, in order to live in this world, another purpose of my working at my job is to make money. And, I hope that YOU will prosper financially because the work of God needs it. I hope God blesses your business. I hope He blesses your investments so that you will have lots of money to give to the Lord's work around the world. The Bible teaches that when we give willingly to the Lord, it's because we love the work of God. When that love is missing, we begrudge what we give to the Lord. We're hesitant. We're reluctant.

* * * * * * * * * * * * * *

REJOICE IN SAYING "THANK YOU" TO GOD

Verse 9 of I Chronicles chapter 29 says,

Then the people rejoiced, for they had offered willingly, because with a loyal heart they had offered willingly to the Lord.

Verse 22 adds,

They ate and drank before the Lord with great gladness on that day.

The third fact is that if you give willingly, you rejoice in the opportunity to say, "Thank you" to God. You rejoice! I don't know if you really get excited at offering time on Sunday morning. "It's now time for the offering. Will the ushers please come forward and we'll have a word of prayer and take the offering."

One of the greatest acts of worship taught in the Bible is bringing your offering to God. Not your tithes. That's taxation. That's required. Tithing is only doing what God requires you to do but when you bring your offering to God, it's one of the greatest acts of worship. It is dealt with over and over in the Psalms and the prophets.

Giving is one of the greatest acts of worship you can perform! Offering time in our church services ought to be very special. You may be so excited with what God has done in your life that you can't wait for those offering plates to be passed. Perhaps you feel like sending a note to the platform to say, "Let's get to the offering earlier in the service. We're waiting too long to take it, and I can't wait! I want to worship the Lord. Let's take it right away. I want to give to God. I've got to have the offering now!" Maybe you are so excited about giving that you want the ushers to pass the plates again.

The first time I preached in a church in Watts, I had a wonderful time. The music was great. The whole service was warm and alive. I preached up a storm, and it seemed like the louder I got, the louder they got. Sometimes I couldn't even remember what I was saying, they were shouting and screaming so much. We were just having a ball. I'd had the opportunity to teach the Pastor in graduate school, and he's doing a great job for God.

One thing I noticed was that they took the offering four times! They had a separate offering for different needs. They just kept taking offerings. They took the last one after the service. They didn't get as much as they wanted so they passed the plates around again!

I decided to kid them a little and said, "You know, maybe you just need to trust God a little more and then one offering would do it." They looked at me amazed and said, "What's the matter, don't you like to give to the work of God?" I felt a little convicted. "Well, uh, yeah. I love the work of God, I put my love gift in the first time." Not to be deterred, he said, "Well, after the message, didn't you want to give again?" Ask yourself, "Do you REALLY REJOICE in the opportunity to express your thanks to God?" Think about it.

Think about what you are giving as it relates to what you have. What you have is totally different from what someone else has and God's not broke. Therefore, the amount isn't critical at all. So, perhaps what you have left is the better barometer of how much you are actually giving.

When you give, do you rejoice? Are you saying, "Thank You" to God? Are you expressing worship and praise to Him?

Offering willingly means that first you understand that
THE WORK IS FOR THE LORD, NOT MAN.
Secondly, you give because
YOU LOVE THE WORK OF THE LORD.
And thirdly, you rejoice in the opportunity
TO SAY, "THANK YOU" TO GOD.

* * * * * * * * * * * * * *

REMEMBER THAT WHAT YOU GIVE ALREADY BELONGS TO HIM

I Chronicles 29:14-16 says,

> *"Who am I, and who are my people,*
> *That we should be able to offer*
> *so willingly as this?*
> *For all things come from You,*
> *And of Your own we have given You.*
> *For we are aliens and pilgrims before You,*
> *As were all our fathers;*
> *Our days on earth are as a shadow,*
> *And without hope.*

O Lord our God, all this abundance that we have prepared to build You a house for Your holy name is from Your hand, and is all Your own."

If you are giving willingly, the fourth principle is that you remember, what you give already belongs to Him. Don't get so enamored with what you give back to the Lord. Stop and think for a moment that everything belongs to Him. "The earth is the Lord's and the fullness thereof." God owns everything! There isn't anything He doesn't own. It's all His!

You may have a car parked in your garage. That's God's car, not yours. But, you use it. There's a man in my church that I go out to lunch with, and he always gives me the keys to his car to drive. That's just his way of reminding himself that the car belongs to God.

You look at what you own and say, "Is that God's or is that mine?" Children grow up playing with their toys and they say, "Mine, mine, mine." You learn early to say, "Mine." But it's really God's. And when you give willingly, you remember that what you give already belongs to Him.

There's a wonderful, old hymn with beautiful words that say, "We give Thee but Thine own." It was written over one hundred years ago.

> "We give Thee but Thine own,
>   whate'er the gift may be,
> All that we have is Thine alone,
>   A trust, O Lord, from Thee.
> May we Thy bounties as stewards true receive,
>   And gladly as Thou blessest us,
>   to Thee our firstfruits give.
> And we believe Thy Word,
>   though dim our faith may be,
> Whatever of Thine own we give,
>   O Lord, we give it unto Thee."

Interesting words from the past. They were giving, meanwhile remembering that what they gave already belonged to the Lord. When you give, remember that what you give already belongs to Him.

* * * * * * * * * * * * * * *

RECOGNIZE THE IMPORTANCE
OF BEING RIGHT WITH GOD

The fifth principle in regard to willing giving is found in verse 17 of I Chronicles 29,

I know also, my God, that You test the heart and have pleasure in uprightness. As for me, in the uprightness of my heart I have willingly offered all these things.

When you give willingly, you recognize the importance of being right with God. There is a sense in which, when you're not right with God, you cannot give willingly.

In the uprightness of my heart I have offered willingly.

Are you right with God? Or is there some secret place in your heart that you're hanging onto and have not let go. Is there something you're doing that's really not right? That will foul up your life tremendously and will affect how you give and how you worship the Lord through giving. Are you right with God?

In Micah chapter six, this Old Testament prophet asked the question,

With what shall I come before the Lord? Will the Lord be pleased with thousands of rams Or ten thousand rivers of oil?

Micah thunders out,

He has shown you, O man, what is good; And what does the Lord require of you But to do justly, To love mercy, And to walk humbly with your God?

Giving willingly to the Lord starts with a heart that is right with God. You recognize the importance of living right with the Lord in order for your offering to be accepted. Some of us use our gifts as an excuse, a justification, for ungodly living. We excuse ourselves by thinking, "But I'm giving to the Lord!"

* * * * * * * * * * * * * * *

COMMIT YOURSELF TO THE LORD BEFORE YOU GIVE

I Chronicles 29:5 says,
"Who then is willing to consecrate himself this day to the Lord?"

If you give willingly to the Lord, you have committed yourself to the Lord FIRST. That's why giving is always a principle of commitment. You respond as you do and give willingly to the Lord because you have already committed yourself to the Lord. In I Corinthians 8:5, it is said of the Macedonian Christians that they had given generously, beyond their ability, during a time of suffering. Paul says, "They first gave themselves to the Lord." That's how they did it!

All giving that is really of God starts with giving yourself to the Lord. Sometimes we sing, "Give of Your Best to the Master." The second stanza says,
"Give Him first place in your heart,
    Give Him first place in your service,
Consecrate every part.
    Give and to you shall be given.
God His beloved Son gave.
    Gratefully seeking to serve Him,
Give Him the best that you have."

Is that true of you? Have you given yourself to God first? I wonder if you have ever made a commitment of your life to God. Have you come to know the Lord as your Savior? If you've come to know the Lord, you can't separate who you are and what you have from your commitment to God.

Have you laid yourself on the altar as Paul described in Romans 12? Have you given your body to God and said, "Lord, I'm Yours - one hundred percent! I want You to use me for Your glory." Has that really happened? Have you given yourself to God?

* * * * * * * * * * * * * *

RETURN ALL OF THE GLORY TO GOD

The final principle we will look at is in verses 20 and 21 of I Chronicles 29.

Then David said to all the congregation, "Now bless the Lord your God." So all the congregation blessed the Lord God of their fathers, and bowed their heads and prostrated themselves before the Lord and the king."

This principle comes last but it is a very important one. When you give willingly, you return all of the glory, all of the blessings and all of the honor to the Lord. When you give willingly, you are expressing worship and praise and honor and blessing.

There are two basic things mentioned in these two verses. One is that you "bless Him." This means that you speak of the worthiness of who He is. You tell Him WHY you're giving to Him and WHY you're praising Him. You're blessing Him for who He is.

Secondly, you bow down to Him. This is submission to His will. The first speaks of His worth. The second is submission to the will of God. Literally, when you give willingly, you are bowing down to Him in submission because you're taking part of what you want to call "mine" (even though it already belongs to Him) and saying, "Lord, this is Yours."

Your gift is something that is vitally connected to who you are. You manage your life by it and you're saying, "Lord, this is Yours. I want to give You a portion of what is already Yours. I want to thank you and to show You that I love You. You're number one in my life. I want to bless You and honor You and praise You."

It has often been said that no matter what you give to God, that which is left will always sustain you better than if you hadn't given.

I have seen it in life consistently. One of the big mistakes we make is failing to see how our money and the way we handle it affects who we are. What we think about our money changes our attitude toward people, toward our service for God, everything. We get so wrapped up in our money. What this fascination with our finances does to us affects everything about us. But you can find financial freedom. You can be free to honor the Lord and you can praise Him even when you know that what you have left doesn't appear to be enough. God will take care of you.

I talked with a woman who's really suffering. She's in a divorce situation, a single parent, unable to pay her bills. She has all kinds of problems. She asked me about giving to the Lord. Now, I want to remind you that I really don't care about the size of the gifts. And I'm not referring to tithing which, in my view, is taxation, not voluntary giving. But, I believe in freewill offerings as a necessary ingredient in our Christian lives.

In talking with her, I said, "In my opinion, no matter how difficult the circumstances, you should still give to God. No matter how broke you are, the money you have belongs to God. Even if what you have doesn't equal all you think you will need, you should still give to God. The amount is not important."

You may say, "That is terrible! What if her expenses are more than what she makes?" Have you ever had that problem? Perhaps you deal with it every month! Sometimes you are tempted to say, "What I give to the Lord would just about pay the rest of my bills." Have you tried it? Have you watched how much bigger the mess gets? We have to go back to a basic principle.

Is the Lord first in your life? Then honor Him. Just keep faithfully giving to God even if the amount is small.

Later, this woman had a particular crisis and told me, "I don't think I can do this." Once again, I encouraged her to "honor the Lord and trust Him for it."

"Easy for you to say," she said. I had to acknowledge, "True. But I do believe you should continue to give."

Not much later, I got a most wonderful letter from her. God had shown her the principle by literally paying off every single debt she had through the gifts of some people who hadn't even known about her problem! She's better off than she's ever been in her entire life!

Do you want to give willingly to the Lord? We all do. Then what's holding you back? Often the reason is ourselves. Those dollars are so tied in with self. Somehow, the green stuff is ME! I pull it out of my pocket and look at it. I say, "That's me! It defines who I am and yet I don't want to admit that money is important. I just won't think about it anymore, but it's me."

WE CAN'T LEAVE IT AT THAT!

What you think about money. . .

How you handle it in your life affects. . .

Your walk with the Lord. . .

Your attitudes toward people. . .

Your desire to help others.

Your entire life is affected by what you do with your money. You can release all that struggle in your heart by:

Giving yourself to the Lord one hundred percent...

lock, stock and barrel.

"All that I am, God, is Yours."

Then, whatever you give Him as an offering is simply an expression of devotion - a simple token that says, "I love You, Lord. I thank You for all You've given me. I want to thank you again and again."

Giving is a commitment to the Lord. Don't ever forget it.

chapter two

HOW MUCH SHOULD YOU GIVE?

The Principle of Sacrifice

When we take giving a step beyond commitment, we find the principle of sacrifice. This is almost a foreign word in the vocabulary of our culture where we are all "well-off" in comparison with the rest of the world. So when we talk about sacrifice, we have a problem in communication.

In regard to "giving," commitment comes first, then sacrifice. In "The Upper Room" daily devotional guide, it says: "Giving is an exercise that makes a healthy heart." That is true. II Corinthians 9:6-15 states it this way,

He who sows sparingly will also reap sparingly,
and he who sows bountifully will also reap bountifully.

So let each one give as he purposes in his heart,
not grudgingly or of necessity; God loves a cheerful giver.

God is able to make all grace abound toward you,
that you, always having all sufficiency in all things,
have an abundance for every good work.

As it is written: He has dispersed abroad,
He has given to the poor,
His righteousness remains forever.

Now may He who supplies seed to the sower, and bread for food, supply and multiply the seed you have sown and increase the fruits of your righteousness, while you are enriched in everything for all liberality, which causes thanksgiving through us to God. For the administration of this service not only supplies the needs of the saints, but also is abounding through many thanksgivings to God, while, through the proof of this ministry, they glorify God for the obedience of your confession to the Gospel of Christ, and for your liberal sharing with them and all men, and by their prayer for you, who long for you because of the exceeding grace of God in you. Thanks be to God for his indescribable gift!

Father, we ask that you will deeply implant upon our hearts what the Bible says as to how we should give. May it not only affect our finances, but may it affect our time and our attitudes towards others as well as our attitudes toward the abilities, talents and gifts You've given us. God teach us to surrender all, let Jesus be the Lord of all.

Thank you in Jesus' name, Amen.

GIVE BOUNTIFULLY

The first principle is give bountifully. You say, "Is that all you've got?" No, there's more. But first, I want to tell you, "Give bountifully." I feel sorry for you if you don't. We just read,

"If you sow sparingly, you reap sparingly, if you sow bountifully, you reap bountifully."

So how much should you give? You'll be glad later on, if you follow my advice. Give bountifully.

YOU REAP WHAT YOU SOW

Obviously, you reap what you sow. You're going to receive in your life what you deserve because of how you've given to the Lord. Is that really true? That message fills the Old Testament, and it's also in the New Testament. What we do affects how we are blessed in the future. How much we give to others affects what we will be given in the future.

This is true because we reap what we sow. If you want great blessings from God in your life, then learn to give all that you are and all that you have to God. Do it generously. Don't hold back. Don't dole out. Don't argue over numbers. Give bountifully of all that you are and all that you have. Make sure you live by the principle that "What I am on earth for is to give myself to the cause of Christ, to His work around the world, to everybody in my life." Be a "giver," not a "taker." Don't concentrate on what you're going to receive. Think of how much you can give. God will take care of the rest. Give bountifully in your life.

Proverbs 11:24 has an interesting thought on this.

"There is one who scatters yet increases more."

In the case of two people making the same income, have you ever wondered why one gives to the Lord and the other doesn't? It often looks to me like the person who gives consistently and regularly to the Lord seems to be able to manage better than the one who doesn't give to the Lord. You can't outgive the Lord! Give bountifully.

There is one who scatters yet increases more; and there is one who withholds more than is right, but it leads to poverty. The generous soul will be made rich, he who waters will also be watered himself.

Look at what Jesus said in Luke 6:38,

Give, and it will be given unto you: good measure, pressed down, shaken together, running over will be put into your bosom. With the same measure that you use, it will be measured back to you.

You reap what you sow. Whatever measure you use to demonstrate your commitment or love for others, that's what is measured back to you, according to the Bible. God's word teaches that principle.

WHEN WE GIVE, GOD IS GLORIFIED

A second reason why we should give bountifully is because God is glorified. I think we make it difficult for people to answer the question, "How do you glorify God?" It's really very simple. It can be speaking, teaching the Word or singing a song. Another way is by what you give.

II Corinthians 9:11 says,

You are enriched in everything for all liberality, which causes thanksgiving to God.

The Jews had what they called the "thank offering."

The administration of this service not only supplies the needs of the saints, but also is abounding through many thanksgivings to God, while, through the proof of this ministry, they glorify God for the obedience of your confession to the gospel of Christ and for your liberal sharing with them and all men.

When you give of yourself, your time and your material things to help the people of God, He is glorified. Thanksgiving goes to God.

Why should you give bountifully? Because you reap what you sow, and because God is glorified. How should you give?

Give bountifully.

GIVE PROPORTIONATELY

And point two, give proportionately. Paul was collecting money for the Jewish believers who were suffering in the land of Judea because of famine. They were ostracized from Jewish society due to their faith in Christ. So, Paul was collecting an offering among Gentile Christians primarily, although some Jews were also in those churches.

GIVE ON THE FIRST DAY OF THE WEEK

I Corinthians 16:1-2 says,

Now concerning the collection for the saints, as I have given orders to the churches of Galatia, so you must do also: On the first day of the week...

They were to give on the first day of the week. You say, "I only get paid twice a month." Divide it by two and take an offering to church with you each week. Maybe you only get paid once a month. Spread it out over four weeks. Sunday is a time to worship and to celebrate, and giving is part of the celebration. "On the first day of the week, let each one of you

lay something aside." Everybody is to be involved in giving.
Everybody can have a part in glorifying God in this manner.

The other side of this directive is that you get to keep some
of your earnings. Aren't you glad? This is not the kind of
"KoolAid and Jim Jones" approach we have seen. You can
keep some of your earnings, but you're going to lay some of
it aside.

There are many groups who say "No, you are to give it all.
That's what they did in the New Testament." In the Book of
Acts, we do see some people making a voluntary contribu-
tion to meet a special need. But, communal living was not
required. Combining all their resources was not a principle
of life. At that time, there was a special need that drew them
together in that way. In their unique situation, they all took
care of each other. The usual principle is, "Lay something
aside -- a portion of what you have."

GIVE AS YOU PROSPER

The next word, as I read it in the New King James says,
"Storing up as he may prosper." What is the standard?
Proportionate giving as you prosper. You always lay aside
some amount. According to this text, we are to "store it up."
If you are Jewish and you say "store it up," you immediately
think of the storehouses in the Temple. Malachi 3, verse 10
says,

> *Bring all the tithes into the storehouse, That there
> may be food in My house. And prove Me now in this...If I will
> not open for you the windows of heaven And pour out for you
> such blessing That there will not be room enough to receive
> it.*

If you grew up in a church where you learned to tithe, perhaps you were taught that the "storehouse" of Malachi chapter 3 is the same as the church. Some churches teach that you

bring your tithes into the local church. Whatever you give to another ministry is over and above the tithe.

I have a problem with that. They seem to be saying that the Jewish Temple of the Old Testament is equivalent to the Church in the New Testament. But the storehouses were only a part of the Temple, so I'm confused by that comparison.

Then there are Christians who say that has no impact whatsoever on us today because they believe I Corinthians 6:19 teaches that "the Temple is our body." We do not have a Jewish Temple, a physical structure anymore. They say, "The Temple is the body of the believer." But the church, too, is called a "temple." The church is called a building and a habitation for God and the symbolism is carried over into the New Testament. Actually, both are taught. My body is a temple of the Holy Spirit, and also the corporate group of Christians is considered to be "the Temple of the Living God."

"Bring all the tithes into the storehouse." Some people say, "That was under the Law." Some books on tithing and giving say that there were three tithes that amounted to approximately twenty percent of a person's income, given every year, and a third tithe given every third year. This one was a built-in welfare system to handle widows and orphans, strangers and non-priestly Levites. So they say, "If you take the third tithe and give it over three years, you're giving about twenty-three and one third percent of your income every year." That's a position held by many Bible teachers.

When I read the Bible and take it for just what it says, I don't see three tithes. I pulled out a giant volume I have, called "The Torah -- a Modern Commentary by the American Hebrew Congregations." This is a standard Jewish resource book. I opened to tithing to read what they had to say. I started laughing! The opening line in the Torah, which is the number one commentary for all Hebrew congregations in this country says, "These verses are baffling." There are a lot of us Gentile Bible teachers who think we understand it. But, the Jewish teachers themselves are not sure what God is saying.

I want to show you what the Bible says and maybe you'll be motivated about proportionate giving. Why does God emphasize tithing and what's the point of it? How much was it, really?

Genesis 14 is the first mention of tithing. It comes four hundred and thirty years before the Law. We're constantly told that we're not under the Law, we're under grace. Still, four hundred and thirty years before the Law, we have tithing mentioned. Nobody taught Abraham to tithe, but he did it.

Then Melchizedek, king of Salem, brought out bread and wine; he was the priest of God Most High. And he blessed him and said:

"Blessed be Abram of God Most High, Possessor of heaven and earth; And blessed be God Most High, Who has delivered your enemies into your hand."

And he gave him a tithe of all(Gen. 14:18).

Four hundred and thirty years before the Law ever said anything about tithing, Abraham is going to give a tithe because he has just had a great victory.

Hebrews chapter 7, in commenting on that Old Testament story in Genesis 14 says,

For this Melchizedek, king of Salem, priest of the Most High God, who met Abraham returning from the slaughter of the kings and blessed him, to whom also Abraham gave a tenth part of all, first being translated "king of righteousness," and then also king of Salem, meaning "king of peace," without father, without mother, without genealogy, having neither beginning of days nor end of life, but made like the Son of God, remains a priest continually.

Verse 4 says,

Consider how great this man was, to whom even the patriarch Abraham gave a tenth of the spoils...now beyond all contradiction the lesser (Abraham) *is blessed by the better* (Melchizedek).

GIVE TO ACKNOWLEDGE GOD'S GREATNESS

Why did Abraham give a tenth? He tithed to recognize the greatness of the Lord. Do you think it is also possible, no matter what the amount of money you give to the Lord, that you are doing the same thing today? Oh yes! Why do we get bogged down in discussing tithing, whether it is ten percent or twenty percent or twenty-three and one third percent? Why is it that we always ignore the purpose behind it, and talk about what the amount was? Why are we so concerned about the amount, when many times Jesus clearly indicated that the amount is not significant at all. What's going on in our hearts is what is important to Jesus.

What is your reason for tithing? Is it to recognize the greatness of the One who blessed you? Has God blessed you?

GIVE TO EXPRESS GRATITUDE FOR GOD'S GIFTS

In Genesis 28, we have the second mention of tithing; that is, giving ten percent of all you have to God. Jacob does an interesting thing here. It seems like he's making a deal with God. Genesis 28:20-22 takes place at Bethel and it says,

Jacob made a vow, saying, "If God will be with me, and keep me in this way that I'm going, and give me bread to eat and clothing to put on, so that I come back to my father's house in peace, then the Lord shall be my God. And this stone which I have set as a pillar shall be God's house, and of all that You give me I will surely give a tenth to You."

Like Abraham, Jacob's promise was made many years before the Law. Yet, Jacob does the same thing Abraham did. Why did Jacob give a tithe? He is displaying his gratitude to God for blessing him. Is that not a valid reason for us to give today? Think again of the reasons, the motives behind biblical giving. One reason was to recognize the greatness of God and another was to express gratitude for the blessing of God.

GIVE TO SUPPORT GOD'S WORK

In Numbers chapter 18 verse 21, we find another reason that people brought tithes.

Behold, I have given the children of Levi all the tithes in Israel as an inheritance in return for the work which they perform, the work of the tabernacle of meeting.

Verse 24:

The tithes of the children of Israel, which they offer up as a heave offering to the Lord, I have given to the Levites as an inheritance; therefore I said to them, "Among the children of Israel they shall have no inheritance."

Verse 28:

Thus you shall also offer a heave offering unto the Lord from all your tithes which you receive from the children of Israel, and you shall give the Lord's heave offering from it to Aaron the priest."

Levites received all the tithes, then they tithed the tithes and gave that to the priests, the sons of Aaron. Everybody tithes. The Levites have no inheritance, they have no land, they have no means of support. Those who worked in the tabernacle leading the services of worship for Israel were supported by the people. They were relieved of the responsibilities of making a living outside their temple services. That's why we have a paid ministry in our churches today. In the late 1800s, a major argument among the denominations raged about having a paid ministry. It was finally settled based on the Old Testament teaching about the priests and Levites being supported because they had no inheritance.

First, the tithe was to recognize the greatness of the Lord.

Second, the tithe was to express one's gratitude for the blessing of God.

Third, the tithe was to provide support for the priests and Levites.

GIVE TO DEMONSTRATE GOD'S POWER

In Deuteronomy chapter 14, verse 23 I read,

You shall eat before the Lord your God in the place where he chooses to make his name abide, the tithe of your grain and your new wine and your oil, the firstlings of your herds and your flocks, that you may learn to fear the Lord your God always.

Tithing shows your reverence for the Lord God and acknowledges your accountability to him. Those who do not consistently and proportionately give something of their income to the Lord are saying with their money that they are not accountable to God.

GIVE TO GET GOD'S BLESSING

At the end of the third year you shall bring out the tithe of your produce of that year and store it up within your gates(Deut. 14:28).

It does not say "in the storehouses of the Temple." It says, "You keep it. Every third year you keep it." What for? There

were non-priestly Levites not serving in Jerusalem but living
in the towns. The people needed these goods to provide for
the Levites who...

*had no proportion or inheritance with you, and the
stranger and the fatherless and the widows who are within
your gates, (so they) may come and eat and be satisfied, that
the Lord your God may bless you in all the work of your hand
which you do.*

In Malachi 3:9,10 God says,

*"You have robbed me, Even this whole nation. Bring all
the tithes into the storehouse, That there may be food in My
House, And prove Me now in this," Says the Lord of Hosts,
"If I will not open for you the windows of heaven   And
pour out for you such blessing That there will not be room
enough to receive it."*

You ask me, "Is it right to give in order that we might be
blessed of God?" Don't just think of tithing in material and
financial ways. What's ahead for believers is far greater than
anything we can possibly possess here on earth. Our reward
will be greater than anything we've experienced here. God
has promised to take care of our needs. The blessing of God
may be much broader than any of us have ever understood.

Why do I give to the Lord?
That I might receive the blessing of God.

GIVE TO WORSHIP GOD

*"And now, behold, I have brought the firstfruits of the
land which you, O Lord, have given me." Then you shall set
it before the Lord your God, and worship before the Lord your
God*(Deut. 26:10).

One of the reasons for bringing your offerings and tithes to God is to worship the Lord. Sometimes when we give our offering, we say that this is vital to our worship time. Paying the light bills is an integral part of our worship service so that we can glorify and praise God. Tithing was necessary in the Old Testament as surely as it is taught in principle in the New Testament. The blessing of God is involved. The worship of God, the praise, the thanksgiving of God Himself is tied to the giving of tithes and offerings.

GIVE TO REJOICE WITH GOD'S SERVANTS

In Nehemiah chapter 12, verse 44 says,

At the same time some were appointed over the rooms of the storehouse for the offerings, the firstfruits, and the tithes, to gather into them from the fields of the cities the portions specified by the Law for the priests and Levites; for Judah rejoiced over the priests and Levites who ministered.

There was rejoicing over those who served! When you give your money to a missionary, pastor, teacher or to support some cause, do you get excited about that person and their ministry? That is one of the great motivations for my wife and me as we give to many people around the world. Joy comes to our hearts thinking of that person and knowing what's going on. We rejoice in the ministry God has given to them, and we want to have a part in it. As you look at these reasons for the tithe, I hope you are saying, "Wait a minute, those are reasons for me to give today."

GIVE SACRIFICIALLY

There's yet another aspect to the proportionate giving we call "tithing." Suppose there's a man who makes $100,000 and another man who makes $10,000. If the man who makes

$10,000 gives ten percent, he gives $1,000 and has $9,000 left to live on. If the man who has $100,000 gives ten percent, he has $90,000 left to live on. If the economy requires $20,000 to live, the man who is left with $9,000 is hurting while the one who has $90,000 is doing fine.

The New Testament says, "As God has prospered you." I think it's wonderful to start with ten percent. But if that's where you stop, you don't understand the New Testament.

"As God has prospered you,"
the Bible says. Has God prospered you?

In the Great American Dream, we keep raising our standard of living "as God prospers us." Materialism is truly a part of us. We are not content with what we have, as Paul wrote about himself. Instead, we enjoy. We go overboard. We consume on ourselves all of the prosperity God has given us to sustain His work around the world.

I've told you to give bountifully.

I've said to give proportionately.

Now, I'm going to tell you to give sacrificially.

A SACRIFICIAL ATTITUDE

Let's think of the story about the widow and her mites (the smallest Jewish coin). What could Jesus buy with two mites? But still He said,

"She has given more than all the rich men who gave out of their abundance, who gave all their tithes, just as the Law demanded. But the woman has given more than them, because she gave all she had."

The question was what she had left, as opposed to the rich men who had a great deal left even though they gave the prescribed amounts.

The willingness to sacrifice is more important than the amount. That's clear from the story in Luke 21 about the widow and two mites. Her attitude was much more important than the amount.

A SACRIFICIAL EXAMPLE

Another reason we should give sacrificially is because that is the way Jesus gave to us. II Corinthians 8:9 says:

You know the grace of our Lord Jesus Christ, that though He was rich, yet for your sakes He became poor, that you through His poverty might become rich.

He gave himself as a sacrifice for us.

Sacrificially, that's the way Jesus gave to us. In I John 3, it teaches us to give the same way. He laid down his life for us. We should be willing to give our lives for others. If you see somebody in need, don't close up your heart to that person.

A wealthy businessman and his pastor went on a missionary trip. One of the countries they went to was Korea. In a rural setting, they came across a very strange sight. It was spring time, plowing time. The missionary, acting as a tour guide, stopped the car. The men got out. The businessman wanted to take a picture of the scene before them.

There was a young man pulling an ancient plow, playing the role of the horse or the mule. Behind the handles of the plow was an elderly man. It was quite a picture! The businessman was fascinated. He said to the missionary, "Those people must be really poor." The missionary said, "I know them very well. Yes, they are poor, but there is more to the story behind this. We built a church here in this village, and they had to raise the money. This elderly man and his son had no money. In fact, a lot of us in the church had been helping them to live. They had no money, but they

wanted to participate in that building program. All they had
was an ox. So they sold the ox and gave the money to the
church. This spring, they're pulling the plow themselves."

The businessman was overwhelmed with this. He said,
"That's a real sacrifice." The missionary said, "They didn't
call it that! They thought it was fortunate that they had an ox
to sell."

It's hard to be an American and talk about sacrifice. How
can we identify with this? We have what we have. Some
have more than others but I'm not interested in how much
you have or how much you give. I am interested in your
knowing the joy and the blessing of a commitment to God
and what He has promised for you in the future. You need to
understand that what you give to God reflects what you really are in your heart more than what you say.

Do you give bountifully and proportionately?

God means so much to you!

You're so faithful and dependable!

You're right on target in your Christian life.

Do you give sacrificially?

Father, thank you for Your Word. We sense the need to re-evaluate where we are in this matter of giving. I pray for those who are thinking through this for the first time or are unfamiliar with Christian truth. Really, in their hearts they do not know, if they died today, whether or not they'd be in heaven with the Lord. Help them to see the sacrifice of Jesus, that He loved them so much He gave Himself as a sacrifice. Christian giving is rooted in His great sacrifice and example. Thank you that salvation was cared for by the death of Christ and His resurrection from the dead. You've asked us to put our faith in what He's already done that we might know the joy of eternity with Him.

Father, I pray that we who are Christians will take a moment to reflect on what we have, that we might make a real commitment in our hearts. Some of us need to start giving proportionately. Some of us need to give sacrificially. Help us to see the connection between giving and our commitment to You.

We thank you in Jesus' name, Amen.

chapter three

WHERE ARE YOU GOING TO GET THE MONEY?

The Principle of Stewardship

We started with the principle of commitment, are you willing to give? Then we moved to the principle of sacrifice, how much should you give? And now we come to the principle of stewardship, where are you going to get the money?

In I Corinthians 4, we have a classic text on stewardship and what's required of stewards. It says in verse one,

Let a man so consider us, as servants of Christ and stewards of the mysteries of God.

Money is not the subject here, but the "mysteries of God." God's revelation in the New Testament is described as a series of mysteries hidden in the Old Testament, now revealed in the New Testament. We're "stewards" of His revelation.

Verse 2 goes on,

"Moreover it is required in stewards (whether the mysteries of God or the management of money for God) *that one be found faithful."*

The New Testament word for stewardship is our English word "economy." It refers to the management of things in any time or culture. It literally means the "law of the house." When a master, the owner of the house is gone, he puts all of his possessions into the hands of the steward, and there are laws that govern the exercise of that steward's role. The "law of the house" then becomes the concept of "economy" or "stewardship."

In I Chronicles 29:10-16, David blessed the Lord before all the congregation, and he said:
"Blessed are you, Lord God of Israel,
our father, forever and ever.
Yours, O Lord, is the greatness,The victory and majesty;
For all that is in heaven and in earth is Yours;
Yours is the kingdom, O Lord,
And You are exalted as head over all.
Both riches and honor come from You,
And You reign over all.
In Your hand is power and might;
In Your hand it is to make great
And to give strength to all.
Now therefore, our God, We thank You
And praise Your glorious name.
But who am I, and who are my people,
That we should be able to offer so willingly as this?
For all things come from You,
And of Your own (hand) *we have given You.*
For we are aliens and pilgrims before You,
As were all our fathers;

O Lord our God, all this abundance that we have prepared to build You a house for Your holy name is from Your hand, and is all Your own.

Communism says that the government owns everything.

Capitalism says that the individual owns everything.

But Bible Christianity says that God owns everything.

Father, I pray that You will deepen our understanding of the role we play as stewards of all that You have given to us. May there be some differences made in our lives because of it. God help us to know that money can be a great blessing or a great burden. Money can either encourage us to walk with God or it can be a hinderance to our followng the Lord. Money can be a trap and a snare or it can be a tool that we can use to glorify Your name. God, help us to understand these principles and apply them we pray.

For Jesus' sake, Amen.

introduction

I want to show you something interesting, maybe even surprising, in that it's located in the Praise Book of Israel. It's a statement regarding stewardship that is repeated in the New Testament. I'm going to give you four statements about stewardship. They are simple things but they help me. I hope they'll help you.

Psalm 49:16 says:

Do not be afraid when one becomes rich, When the glory of his house is increased; For when he dies he shall carry nothing away; His glory shall not descend after him. Though while he lives he blesses himself (For men will praise you when you do well for yourself), He shall go to the generation of his fathers; They shall never see light. Man who is in honor, yet does not understand, Is like the beasts that perish.

Death is the common denominator. You brought nothing into the world, you'll carry nothing out. None of it has even belonged to you during the time you were living, you just think it does. You're trained to say "mine" from childhood. You don't want to share. But all your life is a lesson in stewardship. We are nothing more than stewards of whatever God has given us.

Psalm 50 verse 7-9 says,

Hear, O My people, and I will speak, O Israel, and I will testify against you; I am God, your God! I will not reprove you for your sacrifices Or your burnt offerings, Which are continually before Me. I will not take a bull from your house, Nor goats out of your folds.

God is saying, "I don't have a need. I don't need to take one of your bulls or your goats. I'm thankful for all this that you're giving, but you're not giving it to Me because I need it." God isn't broke. We do not give to Him because He has a need. God already owns it all.

Look at verse 10,
> For every beast of the forest is mine.
> And the cattle on a thousand hills.

We used to sing a chorus,
> "He owns the cattle on a thousand hills,
>   The wealth in every mine"

He does own it! It's all His. Why would He want to take something you've got? He doesn't need it.

> I know all the birds of the mountains,
>   the wild beasts of the field are Mine.
> If I were hungry, I would not tell you.

God is making some sarcastic remarks that they need to hear in order to understand stewardship. He owns it all. He says, "If I was hungry, why would I tell you about it? Do you think you should give because of My need? I have no need, I own everything. The world is Mine and all its fullness." Psalm 24:1 says, *The earth is the Lord's, and all its fullness.*

> Will I eat the flesh of bulls,
>   Or drink the blood of goats?
>   Psalm 50:13

Who eats that? The people who brought the peace offerings ate it. There was a feast where they shared their own gifts that they brought and sometimes they gave to supply the Levites and priests. But, God isn't eating it. They're eating it.

When we give our offerings to God, we say, "Give your offering to God." Sometimes children are confused. "Why are we giving God something? Isn't God going to be able to make it through the week? Why are we giving it to Him?"

It's not because God has a need. We're giving to help other people and God is honored and blessed. But don't get the idea that He has a need. He owns everything. He has simply entrusted some things into your care to manage for a while.

The conclusion is, "Offer to God thanksgiving." The root word behind all giving is to say, "Thank You." Give what you give to God to say, "Lord, this is my thank offering. I just want to thank You for all You've done for me. Here's a portion of my income. It all belongs to You, anyway, so I'm just giving to Your work around the world to say, 'Thank You, Lord, for the way You have blessed my life.' Thank You for salvation; thank You for Jesus; thank You for the breath I breathe. Thank You for flowers; thank You for mountains; thank You for trees. Lord, I've just given You a portion of my income to honor You and to thank You."

> *Offer to God thanksgiving,*
> *And pay your vows to the Most High.*
> *Call upon Me in the day of trouble;*
> *I will deliver you, and you shall glorify Me.*

"I'll take care of you. You don't need to wonder about Me. I'll be there!" God is totally self-sufficient, sovereign, in charge. And everything belongs to Him.

WHAT I HAVE, GOD OWNS

"What I have, God owns." Do you believe that? This is the easiest doctrine in the world to believe and one of the most difficult to apply.

We read it in I Chronicles 29. David said it there. In Psalms, we read it. It's in the Bible over and over. "What I have, God owns."

Your house, your car, your clothes, whatever you have, God owns it. Groceries, everything you have belongs to God. Let's assume that you really believe that. What difference would that make in your life? What is the application of the truth?

In I Corinthians 4, we read the verse about it being "required in stewards that one be found faithful." Paul illustrates this with a problem in the church at Corinth. The church is divided. Some people like Paul, a "teacher"-type. He has a speech impediment. He's a little hard to follow and he's a little guy. You can't see him over the pulpit, but that's all right. Some people like him. He can teach. They listen to Paul.

Then comes Apollos. He is eloquent. People sit there entranced with Apollos. Peter comes, too, and he tears the place apart in his bombastic way, so some follow him. Then there is a group that wants everybody to know how spiritual they are, and they say, "We are of Christ." Paul says all these groups are wrong. They are divided over personalities. Multiple speakers in the church, and they are divided over who they like and who they dislike. You've got to be wondering how Paul is going to use this to illustrate stewardship.

I Cor.4:6,7,

"Now these things, brethren, I have figuratively trans-ferred to myself and Apollos for your sakes, that you may learn in us not to think beyond what is written, that none of you may be puffed up on behalf of one against the other. For who makes you differ from another? And what do you have that you did not receive? Now if you did indeed receive it, why do you glory as if you had not received it?"

If you believe that what you have, God owns; if you believe that every gift, every talent, all you are and have comes from God then there is no room for pride. You'll always have humility and be giving glory to God. There's no room for pride.

How many people do you know who get this proud attitude the moment God blesses them financially. They want you to know, they really had a fantastic year last year. "Of course, we worked our tails off," So what? I know a lot of poeple who "work their tails off" and don't make much money.

Before you know it, there are certain people you can't talk with. There are certain people you've got to associate with. You act differently when you walk into a restaurant. It's amazing what happens to people when they get money.

It doesn't matter whether you have more this year or less, whatever you have, it all belongs to God. So what should be our attitude? Humility. Give God the glory. Praise him. Thank him. You say, "I worked for that!" God gave you the ability to have a job. You never really know that until its taken away from you and you lose your job. God is in absolute control. All that you have and all that you are belongs to the Lord. It doesn't belong to you at all. But He doesn't have a need for it and He's letting you manage it for Him. What I have, God owns so humility, not pride, becomes the principle of my life.

WHAT I NEED, GOD SUPPLIES

Philippians 4:10-20 reads,

I rejoiced in the Lord greatly that now at last your care for me has flourished again; though surely you also did care, but you lacked opportunity.

Not that I speak in regard to need, for I have learned in whatever state I am, to be content:

I know how to be abased, and I know how to abound. Everywhere and in all things I have learned both to be full and to be hungry, both to abound and to suffer need. I can do all things through Christ who strengthens me. Nevertheless you have done well that you shared in my distress.

Now you Philippians know also that in the beginning of the gospel, when I departed from Macedonia, no church shared with me concerning giving and receiving but you only. For even in Thessalonica you sent aid once again for my necessities.

Not that I seek the gift, but I seek the fruit that abound to your account. Indeed I have all and abound. I am full, having received from Epaphroditus the things which were sent from you, a sweet-smelling aroma, an acceptable sacrifice well pleasing to God.

And my God shall supply all your need according to His riches in glory by Christ Jesus. Now to our God and Father be glory for ever and ever. Amen.

My first point is repeated here - God gets the glory since what I have, He owns. Secondly, we see that what I need, God supplies.

It's hard to apply America's "needs" to the other cultures of the world. What I need, God will supply. My God will supply all that every one of you needs.

"My God will supply all my need." When you can pay
your bills and you've got a little extra left over, then you have
an easy time with this. You can serve with such joy! "God
supplies all our needs, it's been a good month." But have you
noticed what happens when you come out a little short, your
MasterCard and Visa are a little high? You have some things
you're not paying. Things are a little tight right now. Maybe
you lose your job or some unexpected expense comes up.
Now you're told, "God will supply all your need."

Do you still believe that God will supply all your need?
According to Paul, this is the time to have contentment.
There's no reason to worry about everything. You say, "You
haven't seen my bank account." There's no reason to worry.
None whatsoever, if you believe that whatever you need God
will supply. He'll take care of you. Paul said, "in whatever
state I am, I've learned therewith to be content." He had no
worry, just sweet contentment.

Look back at chapter 4, verses 6 and 7,

*Be anxious for nothing, but in everything by prayer and
supplication, with thanksgiving, let your requests be made
known to God; and the peace of God, which surpasses all understanding, will guard your hearts and minds through Christ
Jesus.*

Are you contented? Are you happy with God's provision
for you today? You say, "Well, I would appreciate a little increase. I think I could be more contented." We always think
it would be better if we were abounding. But God says
whether you abound or not, you are to be content. Why? Because He will supply.

David said, "I have been young, I have been old, but I have
never seen the righteous forsaken, or his seed begging bread."
You may say to me, "I know that lots of people are starving
in the world, what is the reason for that? Why is it happen-
ing?

Sometimes it is because a given culture has turned its back on the Lord. We ought to help the poor, whether their suffering was brought on by ungodly lifestyles or not. But, I'll tell you something. The Bible says,

My God will supply all your need.

There are illustrations in the Bible which are amazing. There was a widow whose barrel of flour never ran out! The oil in her flask never ran dry! God met her need. And God tells us consistently that He will meet our need.

Our daughter and son-in-law spent a year in Okinawa. They didn't have a bed. They wrote us and said the little church where they were attending was going to get them a bed. They had been sleeping on the floor. They hadn't told us that before. I could have bailed them out. I could have bought them a bed. But, they learned to depend on the Lord. I think that's great!

My Dad always encouraged me to work for what allowance or pay I received and to trust the Lord to meet my needs. He knew something about me. He was a smart man. A lot of parents ruin their kids because they don't think this through. This culture does not really understand that it is God who supplies our needs. We say it. We preach about it. We say "Amen, praise God, brother," but when it comes to saying, "Whatever I need, God will supply," many of us have never been brought to the point of experiencing that. We've just never been put in that position.

The heart of the matter is contentment, not worry. Jesus said, "Don't worry about tomorrow" and yet we spend half our time making our financial plans for, and worrying about tomorrow. He said, "Don't take one thought about it because tomorrow has enough trouble. You're going to wear yourself out worrying about tomorrow and you can't do anything about it."

WHAT I GIVE, GOD MULTIPLIES

**When you remember that what you have,God owns
You learn humility, not pride.**

**When you remember that what you need,God supplies
You learn contentment, not worry.**

People often ask me if I think you should thank the Lord
for your food. I sure do! You should thak Him wherever you
are - at home, in restaurants, wherever you are. You bow your
head and thank God for that food. The Bible tells you to do
that in the book of Deuteronomy. We should thank God constantly. Thanksgiving should pour out of our lives. There need
never be an end to our thanksgiving and blessing the Lord for
all that He has provided no matter where we stand financially.

What I give, God multiplies.

II Corinthians 9, verse 10,

*Now may He who supplies seed to the sower, and bread
for food, supply and multiply the seed you have sown and increase the fruits of your righteousness.*

Here we have the three principles we've already given you
repeated in this little verse:

He supplies seed
WHAT I HAVE, GOD OWNS
Bread for food
WHAT I NEED, HE SUPPLIES
Multiply the seed
WHAT I GIVE, HE MULTIPLIES

Some people think that the phrase, "multiply the seed you've sown" means, "Increase the fruits of your bank account." Is that what it says? No. It says,

Increase the fruits of your righteousness.

God is more interested in how you live than in what you have.

....while you are enriched in everything for all liberality, which causes thanksgiving through us to God. For the administration of this service not only supplies the needs of the saints, but also is abounding through many thanksgivings to God, while though the proof of this ministry, they glorify God for the obedience to the confession of the gospel of Christ, and for your liberal sharing with them and all men.

What I give God multiplies. A lot of people believe that God subtracts. A lot of Christians imply that if you give to the Lord, God literally subtracts. It's sort of like a divine punishment. You give to Him, then God makes it tougher for you to live. I don't read that anywhere in the Bible.

Somebody said to me, "I gave twenty dollars to the Lord! The next day somebody gave me twenty dollars!" Does God give you back exactly what you gave? That isn't what the Bible says! It says He gives back more! It doesn't have to be in this life necessarily. But Jesus said that no matter what you have given in this life, in the life to come He will give you a hundredfold. Whenever you give anything to God (your self, your time, your talent, whatever it is), God always returns more than what you gave. Always. It's just a question of time until you see it.

What I give, God multiplies.

Maybe you still aren't quite sure. This may test your faith somewhat. What I give, God multiplies. I can never outgive the Lord.

Some think that Luke 6:38 says, "Give, and you'll never get anything else for the rest of your life." Of course, it doesn't say that!

Give, and it will be given to you: good measure, pressed down, shaken together, and running over will be put into your bosom. For with the same measure that you use, it will be measured back to you.

The ancient robes were held out to receive wheat as it was poured into them. The picture is that God isn't going to measure out just what you expect but will pour so much into the waiting pouch that it will run over. You won't be able to carry it all home.

Do you really believe that passage? Do you really believe that what you give God literally multiplies either here or in the life to come? The more you get back in this life, the more dangerous your situation becomes because the more God gives you, the more you're accountable for.

To whom much is given, much is required.

So, if you're having a hard time giving now, imagine the struggle you'd have if God gave you more. If He gives you more, you're going to have to give more. You'll have to give more because He's giving more. You say, "Well, I'd like to try it, anyway!" God knows what you're like, start with what you have.

<u>What I have, God owns . . . . . humility, not pride.</u>
<u>What I need, God supplies . . . . contentment, not worry.</u>
<u>What I give, God multiplies . . . . .faith, not doubt.</u>

You must believe that God will multiply your gifts. It's in the Bible. We all know it. Now you're being pressured to use your money as though you believe what you say you believe.

What YOU give, God will multiply.

WHAT I INVEST FOR GOD, HE REWARDS

Mat. 6:19-21 says,

Do not lay up for yourselves treasures on earth, where moth and rust destroy and where thieves break in and steal; but lay up for yourselves treasures in heaven, where neither moth nor rust destroys and where thieves do not break in and steal.For where your treasure is, there your heart will be also.

You brought nothing into this world. You can't carry anything out. There's our stewardship principle again. What you have, God already owns. You're just to manage it. The way you manage it is what puts "treasures in heaven." You're not sending any money on ahead! So, it's how you use your money in giving that is important. How you invest in the lives of others and for the work of God is what stores up "treasures in heaven where your heart is." What God says is, "Don't say your heart's in heaven if, in fact, you haven't laid up treasures there because where your treasure is, there's your heart."

In chapter 25 of Matthew there is a story of some men who have given talents. They are to be stewards of what was given to them. One had five talents, one had two and one had one. What we invest for the Lord and in his work, God will always reward.

After a long time the Lord of those servants came and settled accounts with them. So he who had received five talents came and brought five other talents, saying, "Lord, you delivered to me five talents; look I have gained five other talents besides them." His lord said to him, "Well done, good and faithful servant; you were faithful over a few things, I will make you ruler over many things. Enter into the joy of your Lord."

*He also who had received two talents came and said,
"Lord, you delivered to me two talents; look, I have gained
two more talents besides them." His Lord said to him, "Well
done, good and faithful servant; you have been faithful over
a few things, I will make you ruler over many things. Enter
into the joy of your Lord."*

*Then he who had received the one talent came and said,
"Lord, I knew you to be a hard man, reaping where you have
not sown, and gathering where you have not scattered seed.
And I was afraid, and went and hid your talent in the ground.
Look, there you have what is yours."*

*But his lord answered and said to him, "You wicked and
lazy servant, you knew that I reap where I have not sown, and
gather where I have not scattered seed. Therefore you ought
to have deposited my money with the bankers, and at my coming I would have received back my own with interest.*

*"Therefore take the talent from him, and give it to him who
had ten talents. For to everyone who has, more will be given,
and he will have abundance; but from him who does not have,
even what he has will be taken away.*

*"And cast the unprofitable servant into the outer darkness.
There will be weeping and gnashing of teeth."*

A lot of people struggle with this passage. They say, "Is
this teaching us to work for our salvation?" No. What it is
saying is that every one of us is a steward of what God has
given us. What you invest, God rewards. You're to lay up
treasures in heaven. But the fact is, a lot of us have not done
that. We have kept it for ourselves. Even though we know
that we brought nothing into the world and we can't take anything out, we're keeping it for ourselves. We are not invest-
ing it. We're not laying up treasures in heaven, we're laying
up treasures on earth. We're programmed to do that in our

society. What a tragedy.

It's easy to say you believe in Jesus and you want to go to heaven. You want to make sure of that. But how do you demonstrate in your life that you believe that? Do you believe God is going to reward you in heaven? The Bible speaks about it continuously yet we never do anything about it. Are you doing anyting about it?

Don't misunderstand. There's only one way to get to heaven and that is by faith in Jesus Christ and His death on the Cross and His resurrection from the dead. What we're talking about here is whether or not we who say we believe what He says, in fact really do believe it. God teaches that if you believe in Jesus, your treasure and your heart is in heaven. That's what you're really looking forward to. You're not hung up on things down here. They come and go.

God takes care of you. What we need, God supplies. Everything I've got, God owns anyway. So, there's no room for pride or boasting, self-confidence or worldly security. Your confidence is in the Lord and you're looking forward to meeting Him. You want to hear these sweet words,

Well done, thou good and faithful servant, enter thou into the joy of thy Lord.

And, you're not giving because He's broke. He doesn't need anything. He's got it all.

In Luke 16, there's an unjust steward. The fellow was not a believer and he didn't do right. Then he straightened up. In verse 9, we read,

I say to you, make friends for yourselves by unrighteous mammon (money), *that when you fail, they may receive you into everlasting habitations. He who is faithful in what is least is faithful also in much; and he who is unjust in what is least is also unjust in much. Therefore if you have not been faithful in unrighteous money, who will commit to your trust the*

*true riches? And if you have not been faithful in what is
another man's, who will give you what is your own? No servant can serve two masters; for either he will hate the one
and love the other, or else he will be loyal to the one and
despise the other. You cannot serve God and money.*

Is money controlling you or are you being controlled by
God and using your money freely to bless God's work around
the world? That's a simple point but I think that it's possible
that by the way you use your money, you are demonstrating
that you have no heart for God in heaven.

That is a serious matter. What I invest, God rewards. The
lesson here is faithfulness, not neglect of the things of God.
Not like the steward who hid his talent. The question is,
"What has God given me to be faithful in?" The more we
have, the more we are accountable to God.

Where will you get the money to support God's work?
"Everything I have, God already owns." So you can only give
Him what you have. Some people make commitments of
what they don't have, hoping to receive it. Sometimes that's
confused with "faith promise" giving. You may make a
promise to God to give Him something, but what you have
doesn't even belong to you. It belongs to the Lord. You may
make a commitment by faith to give it because you don't
know how you can give it and also pay your bills. There I
can see an issue of trust. You know that what you need God
supplies.

You are faced with the next step in giving. Is God sub-
tracting or multiplying? He says He's multiplying. Therefore, what you invest in the work of God, God will reward.
Why would you want your treasure here? You didn't bring
anything into the world and you're not taking anything with
you when you leave. What you want is treasure in heaven.
True riches are based on your helping to spread the Gospel

around the world. Every time you bring an offering to God, you're saying, "Thank you, Lord, for all You've done for me."

What I have, God owns.
What I need, God supplies.
What I give, God will multiply.
What I invest, God rewards.

Father, thank You so much for Your Word. I pray that You would help us to get a clear picture of this matter of our finances. Lord, I thank You that Jesus gave His life on the Cross that we might live forever. I know, Father, that You have used the Word of God to challenge us to give the best that we can to honor the Lord and glorify Him. I pray, Lord, that You will cause those who have never really begun to make a commitment to Jesus Christ to see that's where it starts. God, teach them that only through Jesus Christ, our Lord and what He did on the Cross can we ever hope to be saved. Show them that our sin was paid for by His death nineteen hundred years ago. We thank you that He's a living Savior who rose from the dead. You told us if we believe that, we will be saved. God, help us to begin by giving our hearts to You and teach us all to trust You and to obey You.

In Jesus' name, we pray. Amen.

chapter four

WHY SHOULD YOU GIVE?

The Principle of Motivation

Thus far, we've talked about the principle of commitment,
ARE YOU WILLING TO GIVE?

Then we talked about the principle of sacrifice,
HOW MUCH SHOULD YOU GIVE?

We went into the tithing problem of the Old Testament, and how, though it was a taxation under Israel, the real reasons people tithed weren't much different from the reasons we give today.

We also discussed the fact that the amount is not important. God's not broke. What is important is being faithful in giving an expression of thanksgiving to God.

We have also talked about the principle of stewardship.

EVERYTHING YOU HAVE, GOD OWNS

EVERYTHING YOU HAVE, GOD OWNS

I think a lot of us are up tight with money. One man found my teaching on giving took him to conclusions he couldn't handle so he wrote me a letter:

"Dear David,

"I know that God owns all I have. But does that mean that if someone meets me in a parking lot and wants the keys to my car, I give them to him, and I tell him he's welcome to the car because it belongs to the Lord anyway? And if he takes it, the Lord will provide me with another one, won't he? Should I offer him some gas money too? By the way, if he doesn't speak English, how will he understand? Does it follow that if all I have belongs to God, I shouldn't carry insurance either? I mean, that's the law of the land, but am I trusting my insurance company instead of the Lord? If I purchase the insurance, am I saying I don't trust God, so now I'm robbing God of a chance to show His power and glory in my life by carrying insurance?

"In Scripture, it says that if anyone asks for your cloak, give him your coat also. Well, isn't that like giving them your house, because shouldn't that be their shelter against the cold of the night? I'm a renter and not a homeowner. I don't have a house to give away, or to turn over to a thief, but all this ownership thing is literally keeping me awake.

"I have another question. In relinquishing a possession to a thief, am I really contributing to crime by allowing the thief to take my possession which belongs to the Lord. It also follows, if someone threatens my life, to get my car or whatever, then I should say, 'Take my car, my money and my life because Jesus is my Lord, and I'm going to heaven anyway, so I won't need all this stuff.'"

This person is not being critical, this person is very concerned about the whole thing. This surely causes us to re-examine what we do and why we do it. In light of faith in the

Lord Jesus, it seems to me that believing that "What I have, God owns" makes great changes, lots of them, in our lives.

Maybe you have questions about stewardship in regard to the car illustration that I used. Perhaps somebody wanted to use your car and suddenly you got a little antsy about that. It could be that you own a Mercedes or a Rolls-Royce. If you own an old, beat up station wagon that barely makes it to the store and back, do you find it easier to say, "It's yours, Lord!" We're ready to give that to the Lord's work.

Wait a minute, although God possesses everything, you're a steward of all that He allows you to use. In fact, the Bible teaches that you are to manage what He gives you and be responsible for it as though you were the owner. In fact, the Bible teaches private ownership and tells you that you're responsible for how you use it. Don't take stewardship to mean that nothing belongs to you in any sense at all. Oh yes, it does! Everything is the Lord's but a steward, biblically and in ancient times, is just like an owner. He is held accountable by the owner. The steward can make any decision he wants to about management of what he's given. He's the controller. He has to invest. He has to decide on things like insurance and he is held accountable for things like that.

You don't take your hands off the wheel of the car while you're on the freeway so that you can really trust the Lord to take care of you. The Bible says,

Keep back thy servant from presumptuous sins.

You're responsible to manage your time and your money. You should not give indiscriminately to everybody who asks it of you. There are also principles on that in the Bible. Yet, on the other hand, the pendulum has swung so far to the side of not recognizing that God owns everything that many people don't give to Him because they forget that

What we have, God owns.

Someone else wrote asking where in the Bible it teaches
that what we have is really ours to manage as we see fit. Turn
to Acts 5 where we have an example of this in a man and his
wife, Ananias and Sapphira. These two people had some
property which they decided to sell. A lot of Christians were
bringing gifts to the apostles. It was not exactly communal
living, communistic or socialistic, but they were bringing
things to help everybody in the group because some didn't
have any money. The apostles were distributing it to those
who had need. So, Ananias and Sapphira decided to bring
their gift, too.

Now what's the problem here? In verse 2 we read,

*He kept back part of the proceeds, his wife also being
aware of it, and brought a certain part and laid it at the
apostles' feet.*

There's the situation. Now watch what happens.

*But Peter said, "Ananias, why has Satan filled your heart
to lie to the Holy Spirit and keep back part of the price of the
land for yourself? While it remained, was it not your own?
And after it was sold, was it not in your own control?"*

There's your answer. There is a matter of private ownership, but we are responsible to God who is the ultimate owner
of everything that we have. Even when he sold it and got the
money, Ananias could manage it as he saw fit. Their giving,
in that situation, was for the purpose of meeting the need at
hand. The believers were suffering deeply and those who
could were making a voluntary decision to share what they
had. While they had the property, it was their own, they didn't
have to sell it. When they sold it, they got the money. That
was all their own, too. It was still in their control.

The problem was that they lied about how much money
they were giving. It was the lying, not the fact that it all
belonged to God and none of it belonged to them that was the
issue. I believe in voluntary giving because what you have

belongs to you in the sense that we're all stewards who act just like owners. We are running our affairs according to the "laws of the house" and we are to manage our entire "economy." We are to make wise decisions, we're to invest. God isn't against investments. As a matter of fact, Jesus taught that wise stewards are to be commended for good investments. God understands private ownership.

We need to be careful, however, about our attitudes, Be sure you don't think, "It's mine" when you brought nothing into this world, and you're not taking anything with you when you leave. "The earth is the Lord's and the fullness thereof." We're just stewards managing things for Him. How we manage is a very critical matter.

WHY SHOULD YOU GIVE?

There are seven reasons I would like to suggest as to why you should give. Perhaps you should write them down and place them where you will look at them often. I hope that these thoughts will begin to control and affect your giving patterns. Our best motivation for giving comes from the Bible.

I don't believe that I motivate anybody to give. I believe you are motivated yourself. You're either motivated to do something about the needs that reach your ears or you're not moved to do anything about it. The reason we teach the Bible is so we will be motivated by what the Bible teaches. Every one of us is motivated, either to do something or not to do it, either to turn a message into action or not to apply it. I don't motivate you, I only inform you of what God's Word says and, if that doesn't reach your heart, nothing I say will make any difference. Every one of us is motivated one way or the other and, hopefully, we're motivated to do right because of what God says in His Word.

I could try to motivate you on the basis of fear, but I don't believe in that. I believe in recognizing the sovereignty and greatness of God. I don't believe in being afraid that if I don't give, God will judge me and I'll lose my job. I could try to motivate you in a lot of other ways, but I want you to see why God says you should give. I want to give you reasons from the Bible that motivate me to give but, before God, you are going to have to make the decision as to whether or not you give.

I WANT TO SUPPORT THE WORK OF THE GOSPEL

Supporting the work of the Gospel is a major motivation in my life. Romans 10 verse 14 says,

How then shall they call on Him in whom they have not believed? And how shall they believe in Him of whom they have not heard? And how shall they hear without a preacher? And how shall they preach unless they are sent?

We must support those who go and send them where they are needed.

When a person tells me God is calling them to work full-time to some country, do they deserve my support?

In I Corinthians 9:3 Paul says,

My defense to those who examine me is this: Do we have no right to eat and drink?

The grammar in the Greek is stronger than in the English but the point is obvious in both languages.

Do we have no right to take along a believing wife, as do also the other apostles, the brothers of the Lord, and Cephas? Or is it only Barnabas and I who have no right to refrain from working? Who ever goes to war at his own expense? Who plants a vineyard and does not eat of its fruit? Or who tends a flock and does not drink of the milk of the flock?

Do I say these things as mere man? Or does not the law say the same also? For it is written in the law of Moses, 'You shall not muzzle an ox while it treads out the grain.' Is it oxen God is concerned about? Or does He say it altogether for our sakes?

For our sakes, no doubt, this is written, that he who plows should plow in hope, and he who threshes in hope should be partaker of his hope. If we have sown spiritual things for you, is it a great thing if we reap your material things? If others are partakers of this right over you, are we not even more? Nevertheless we have not used this right, but endure all things lest we hinder the gospel of Christ.

Do you not know that those who minister the holy things eat of the things of the temple, and those who serve at the altar partake of the offerings of the altar? Even so the Lord has commanded that those who preach the gospel should live from the gospel.

I believe in a paid ministry because the Bible teaches it. Some ministers can have a job to sustain them. Sometimes it is best. Paul was tentmaker. But the fact is, the Bible teaches that those who proclaim the Gospel should live from the Gospel. Ministering demands full-time effort. There are some people who pastor local churches. There are people who work with a church or mission as support ministries. They deserve our support.

But many people in this country are supporting works that do not proclaim the Gospel of Christ in actuality. I don't know if you're bothered about it, but it bothers me. A pastor back East came to me to say that he was very concerned about his financial status. His church was not supporting him. He thought he was going to have to get a job. I asked him about his schedule and he told me what he did. He didn't mention studying the Bible and preaching. So, I said, "How much time do you spend looking into the Bible and preparing messages?"

He answered, "That isn't necessary because our denomination sends us an outline. It only takes me about twenty minutes to get it ready for Sunday."

I said, "You don't deserve a penny of support because you aren't in the Word of God. What do you think pastors are supposed to do?"

He said, "You know, I've wondered about that for years!"

I've been to mission fields and I've met missionaries who aren't doing one thing for the Gospel. But, one man I know builds buildings to provide adequate centers for missionaries who are proclaiming the Gospel because he really believes he's part of getting the Gospel out. He's worth supporting in my judgment. I believe in that secretary who goes and helps a missionary in some jungle so that they can tell more people about Jesus. But if they're involved in supporting ministries that do not proclaim the Gospel, I don't want to give to them. I'm as serious as I can be. People are supporting works that don't deserve to be supported.

On the other hand, a lot of missionaries don't know how to tell you that they need help. Should missionaries tell us what their financial needs are, so we can support them? On the basis of what Paul wrote in I Corinthians 9, I say, "Absolutely!"

Missionaries sometimes suffer because they have serious financial needs but they feel that if they shared their need, they would not be "spiritual." Paul made it very clear in this chapter that one of the responsibilities we have is to send people out to proclaim the Gospel of Christ. We must be sure that their needs are met. The Bible commands us to support them. That's why I give.

As a principle, HOW I GIVE is that ten percent of what I make goes to a local ministry. I'm not legalistic and I'm not into tithing. I just believe that the principle of setting aside the firstfruits has not changed. So I give ten percent where I worship. In addition to that, I like to support many other ministries. There are commitments Carole and I have made to missionaries and other enterprises.

I love to support the work of the Gospel. The more you think about it, the more you want to do it. I like what radio is doing. I like what television is doing. They get the Word of God out and people are coming to Christ. I want to support that.

Recently, my wife and I were signing books at a bookstore where there were several authors who have radio ministries. Carole was enamored with one author in particular. He was signing books. I know him. He has a radio ministry but I won't mention his name because you know him, too. He was talking about a letter he had just sent out. Carole said to him, "Oh yes, I got that this week!" I couldn't believe it but she knew exactly what the letter was all about. I said, "That's interesting! Do you follow his ministry?" She answered, "I support him. I send him some support from the grocery money." From the money Carole gets, she wants to give, too. Any Christian, whoever you are, a child in a family or a wife or a husband, if you love the Lord, you want to support His work.

I WANT TO HELP OTHERS IN TIME OF NEED

The problem in a materialistic culture is that it's hard to know who is really in need. But there are many people in need in this country and around the world. And God teaches us to give to the poor. Sometimes we're fooled into giving where there is no need. But I'd rather you have an attitude that's right and sometimes get ripped off than to be so cautious you never give money to help anybody.

I don't know how you handle this, mentally and emotionally, but here's how I handle it. I set aside money that I can give to help somebody. I don't want anybody telling me who I should help. I want to be in control. I want to be able to help people on the basis of what I feel led to do. The Bible teaches us to give to people who are in need. There's no doubt about it. Ephsians 4:28 says,

Let him who stole steal no longer, but rather let him labor, working with his hands what is good, that he may have something to give to him who has need.

Why should I make money? God says it is to help people who are in need.

Passages about giving to the poor are abundant in the Old Testament and there are several in the book of Proverbs. God tells us that He will bless us enormously if we give to the poor. James 2:15-17 says,

If a brother or sister is naked and destitute of daily food, and one of you says to them, "Depart in peace, be warmed and filled," but you do not give them the things which are needed for the body, what does it profit? Thus also faith by itself, if it does not have works, is dead.

In I John 3:17-18, we read,

Whoever has this world's goods, and sees his brother in need, and shuts up his heart from him, how does the love of God abide in him? My little children, let us not love in word or in tongue, but in deed and in truth.

Can anything be more clear? If we shut our hearts against somebody that has a need when we have the means to help them, God says, "How does the love of God dwell in your hearts?" What we're talking about is very practical.

What we do with our money is as critical as what we say as committed disciples of Christ. Too many of us have been separating the secular from the sacred and one of the secular items has been money. To a Christian, all things are sacred.

I WANT TO RECEIVE A HEAVENLY REWARD

A lot of believers do not like to be motivated on the basis of incentive. We don't like to tell small children, "If you will memorize this verse, I'll give you a candy bar." We'd feel better if we said, "I'll give you a New Testament." Either way, we're using incentives. We've just changed the incentive a bit and made it more spiritual. Is incentive or reward used in the Bible to motivate me to give? Oh, yes! Over and over again. We've been playing down the reward system of the Lord. We've put it in the camp of carnality. We feel it's more Spirit-filled to say, "I just leave it to the Lord. I'm not working for a reward. I work because I love Him."

Jesus never made that kind of dichotomy. Work and reward were always together. Do we in fact work for heavenly reward? Jesus said to the rich young ruler in Matthew 19:2,

Go, sell what you have and give to the poor, and you will have treasure in heaven; and come, follow me.

Does the Bible teach there's treasure in heaven? In Matthew 6:20, Jesus says,

Lay up for yourselves treasures in heaven, where neither moth nor rust destroys and where thieves do not break in and steal.

There's much in the Bible about this subject as you know if you're familiar with the Word of God. The question is what we believe about it. I believe in taking God literally and I'm looking forward to receiving a heavenly reward. I try not to be carnal, but rather to be motivated because of love of the Lord and His work. But whatever my personal motivation, the Bible says that we are to give because He will reward us in the future.

I'm more than a little upset with the "health/wealth" gospel of today. The prosperity message we hear today is not true the way it's presented in most cases. Why? Because God is not saying that if I give down here, I will reap here on earth. That is not what He's saying. If God blesses you, you are not to conclude that it's because you did the right thing. Spirituality is not based on whether you are being blessed materially or not, because the Bible consistently teaches that it is the wicked that we usually see prospering. If you are prospering, maybe you should be quiet about it. It is not a sign that you are walking with the Lord any more than it is a sign that you're not walking with the Lord.

If God decides to bless you, what's His reason for it? He wants you to have more to give to help His cause around the world. We aren't to lay up treasures down here. The kind of gospel that says, "You give to us and then God will bless you here" is not God's message. God will bless you all right but He's talking about spiritual rewards.

Proverbs 19 tells us that when you give to the poor, you are actually lending to the Lord and He will return it in the future. The Bible tells us that everything you have given to Him now, He will reward a hundredfold in the life to come. Every cup of cold water given, every kindness, will be rewarded. He is righteous and will not forget your work and the labor of love which you've shown ministering in His Name.

Look at what God says in I Timothy 6:17,

Command those who are rich in this present age not to be haughty, nor to trust in uncertain riches but in the living God, who gives us richly all things to enjoy. Let them do good, that they be rich in good works, ready to give, willing to share, storing up for themselves a good foundation for the time to come, that they may lay hold on eternal life.

Does that last phrase refer to salvation? No. You're not saved by giving your money. That statement deals with your understanding of the real issues and priorities in life. The way you use your money tells me whether or not you have a firm grasp on the real issues of eternal life.

Do you value eternal life so much that it affects how you use your money? That's the point of the passage. He's warning those of us who have lots of things, not to trust in them but to be willing to give some away and to share them. This way you're building something for the future in the life to come. You're going to be with the Lord in heaven forever so everything you do here on earth should focus on the ultimate objective of being with Him. The way you handle your money tells the story of whether you really believe that or not.

I GIVE BECAUSE:

I want to support the work of the Gospel.

I want to help those in need.

I want to receive a heavenly reward.

and fourthly, I give because:

I WANT MY FAITH IN GOD'S SUPPLY TO GROW

I'd like to illustrate something for you. Decide what you want to give to the Lord. Remove that amount of money from every paycheck however much it is. Just completely remove it. The amount is between you and the Lord. This is what I do. It has been extremely helpful in my life. If it helps you, praise the Lord. I remove the amount I've decided on. I do not take my whole check. Then I figure out my budget based on the balance of the check. You can do it, too. Whatever you give to the Lord, remove it, and whatever remains, consider that to be one hundred percent. Even though this is so simple, it is critical because through television ads, radio, magazines, and many other things we experience daily, we're programmed to save up for some future date, retirement or whatever. But if I do that and I don't give on a consistent basis, I wind up using it for something other than the Lord's work. So every month, whenever I get my check, I put the part I've decided on aside and I manage the rest as though it were one hundred percent of my income.

Maybe you are in a kind of business where your income fluctuates from month to month. Nevertheless, God teaches systematic, regular, faithful giving out of what we actually receive. You'll have to trust God that He will meet your need no matter what changes you experience. You see, we're being tested every time we give, especially when we're not sure we can manage on what's left. We're giving and we must have faith in God's supply.

There have been times when the amount of money that I now treat as one hundred percent has not been adequate to pay what I owe. I can't manage my life on what's left. "What do you do then?" you ask. You have a couple of choices. You can pray that God will send you enough additional money to make it. Or you can reduce your standard of living. You may find this hard to believe but I have had great joy in making those decisions in my life. Great joy! I think these choices are great because sometimes you have to say, "We can't do that. Maybe later, but we can't do that now. We'll have to wait even though that's not 'American.'"

Maybe you've got it all together and this seems simple. But the majority of believers are struggling with finances. It doesn't matter how much you make. It really doesn't. The more money that comes in, the more trouble we can have.

You need to develop faith. Look at II Corinthians 9:8 where it says,

God is able to make all grace abound toward you, that you, always having all sufficiency in all things, have an abundance for every good work.

That's His promise.

I believe it.

My God shall supply all your need.

Philippians 4:19

I WANT TO SAY, "THANK YOU" TO GOD

II Corinthians 9:11-12:

You are enriched in everything for all liberality, which causes thanksgiving through us to God. . . . . Also abounding through many thanksgivings to God.

Verse 13:   *They glorify God.*

Do you want to glorify God? Do you want to give thanks to Him? That's a motivation for giving. Every time you give, you are saying, "Thank you" to the Lord. Sometimes I hear negative attitudes about offerings. Sometimes Christians act as though we're not supposed to discuss money. There's a great deal in the New Testament about money. We need to examine our attitude about what the Bible says about money. I look at giving as a key opportunity to express thanks to God.

A lady wrote to me and said, "I've never seen you put anything in the collection plate when you're on the platform."

Let me tell you what Carole and I do. We prepare an envelope privately and I don't bring it up on the platform with me. I was taught to do that in seminary! Seriously, they discussed it in class and suggested that you should take it up on the platform with you and make it visible to everyone. The idea was that others would be motivated by my example. We have three services in our church. Now what shall I do? Take my envelope back and put it in again for the second service and the third? It's amazing what people think.

I could write three checks, I suppose, but I really believe it's between me and God. I don't need to explain what I do to you and you don't need to explain what you do to me. But we both need to rememebr that

all things are open and naked under the eyes of Him with whom we have to deal.

It's between you and the Lord. And giving should be a thing of joy, not guilt trips.

I believe everybody is motivated by what they understand from God's word in their own heart. I believe they are going to do what they're going to do, regardless of what I do or say.

I WANT TO EXPERIENCE JOY

If your heart is right, and you know what you're doing, giving is a joyous thing. I get great joy when I support a missionary and he sends me a prayer letter telling me about a half-naked indian in the jungles that he led to Jesus Christ! I get really excited about it! I'm thankful I could give to help that missionary go there and tell that man that Jesus died for him. Joy ought to be in our hearts because of the work of the Lord. I love to give.

Our giving shouldn't be based on whether there is a financial need or not, either. That's a moot question. That's not the issue here. Your whole life and Christian experience may be more exposed here than you expected. You may want to push these thoughts away from you to avoid any changes in your lifestyle. But there is so much to be gained by facing your motivations in giving to the Lord.

One of the great things about giving is to experience joy. In I Chronicles 20:17 David says,

Now with joy I have seen your people, who are present here to offer willingly to You.

Verse 22 adds,

So they ate and drank before the Lord with great gladness on that day.

Giving should not fill your heart with sorrow, upset feeling, bitterness, hesitation or reluctance. There should be joy in our hearts over the privilege of giving to God and His work.

I WANT TO EXPRESS MY SUBMISSION TO GOD

In Genesis 14, Abraham gave a tenth of everything that he took in battle. It wasn't because he knew about tithing. Tithing wasn't taught for four hundred years after that. Abraham gave his tithe to recognize the greatness of the One who had blessed him. That is clearly conveyed in Hebrews chapter 7.

The lesser is blessed of the greater.

Abraham recognized the greatness of the One who had blessed him and by returning part of the spoils to Him, honored Him.

Proverbs 3:9,10 promises,

Honor the Lord with your possessions, And with the first fruits of all of your increase; So your barns will be filled with plenty, And your vats will overflow with new wine.

Honor the Lord! Demonstrate your submission to Him and acknowledge His sovereignty over all. Make sure everyone knows you believe that everything belongs to Him. You're only a steward of what He has given you.

Money is not sinful in and of itself but the possession of it doesn't guarantee spirituality, either. It's a tool to use. It is not a master to control you. When you love and pursue money as a goal in life, it will cause many problems. God says so. The most dangerous things I see are the following:

1) Money becomes more important to you than the treasures of heaven.

2) Money gives you a false sense of security.

The worlds of media and business are promoting the false idea that money provides security. It comes at us in volumes every day. But money can only give us a false sense of security. Our security is that GOD will supply what we need.

3) Money can keep you from following Jesus Christ with all your heart.

That's the most dangerous thing of all about money. There are several examples in the Bible of people who lost out completely in their relationship with Jesus Christ because they loved their money too much. It can keep you from total commitment to Christ.

Father, I know that perhaps these things seem new and demanding. Maybe we're having problems in our relationship withYou. Some may be reading here that do not know if they'd be in heaven with You if they died today. They've never made a personal commitment to Jesus Christ. I pray that they will start today to walk the path of discipleship with You. May they believe in Christ before it is too late.

Help us all Father, as we think about money, to evaluate what it means in regard to our commitment to You and Your work.

Thank you in Jesus' name, Amen.

A PERSONAL NOTE FROM DAVID HOCKING:

What changes do you intend to make after reading this book?

Are you satisfied with your present habits of giving?

Do they reflect biblical teaching?

Do they reflect your love of the Lord?

Do they reflect your commitment to His work?

Biblical giving is beautifully summarized in II Corinthians 9:7,8. Why not memorize these verses and take a moment right now to ask God to speak to your heart about what you should do with your finances!

So let each one give as he purposes in his heart,
Not grudgingly or of necessity;
for God loves a cheerful giver.
God is able to make all grace abound toward you,
That you, always having all sufficiency in all things,
have an abundance for every good work.

BIOLA HOUR SPECIAL EDITION

THE BIOLA HOUR, a half hour daily broadcast sponsored by BIOLA UNIVERSITY, La Mirada, California, is heard on a special network of radio stations across the United States and Canada.

Dr. David Hocking, who explores into the biblical principles about giving in this new book, PASSING THE BUCK, follows a long tradition of speakers and Bible teachers who have been featured on the BIOLA HOUR.

When Dr. Louis T. Talbot became President of Biola and sensed that radio, though in its infancy then, held tremendous potential for future ministry, he began a daily radio broadcast. The date was November 16, 1932 and the program was later to become THE BIOLA HOUR.

It has continued ever since, making it one of the oldest daily religious radio broadcasts in the nation.

BIOLA UNIVERSITY in La Mirada, traces its beginnings to 1906. Still today, it continues to equip Christian young people, through Bible-centered education, for productive lives in service for Christ as professionals, in the pulpit, on the mission field or in the work place.

For further information about THE BIOLA HOUR, write

BIOLA MINISTRIES, 13800 BIOLA AVENUE
LA MIRADA, CALIFORNIA 90639